MONSTER FIGHT CLUB
OUTLAWS AND VILLAINS FROM HISTORY

ANITA GANERI   AND DAVID WEST

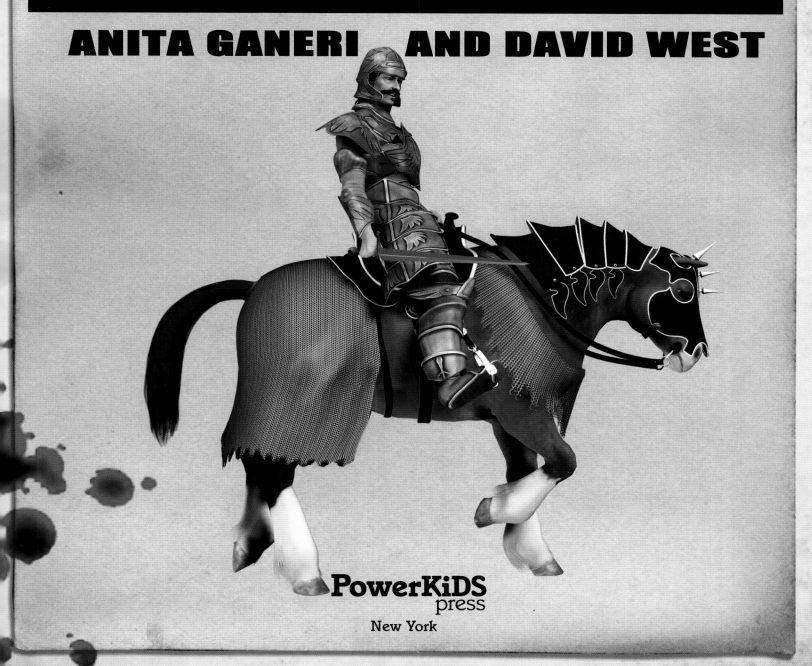

PowerKiDS
press

New York

Published in 2012 by The Rosen Publishing Group, Inc.
29 East 21st Street, New York, NY 10010

Designed and produced by
David West Books

Designer and illustrator: David West
Editor: Ronne Randall
U.S. Editor: Kara Murray

Library of Congress Cataloging-in-Publication Data

Ganeri, Anita, 1961–
Outlaws and villains from history / by Anita Ganeri and David West.
p. cm. — (Monster fight club)
Includes index.
ISBN 978-1-4488-5199-7 (library binding) — ISBN 978-1-4488-5236-9 (pbk.) —
ISBN 978-1-4488-5237-6 (6-pack)
1. Outlaws—History—Juvenile literature. I. West, David, 1956– II. Title.
HV6441.G36 2012
364.1092'2—dc22

2011003073

Manufactured in China

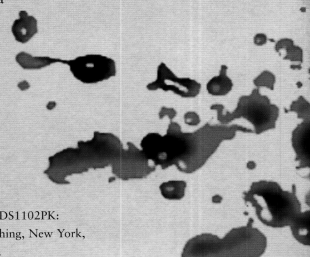

CPSIA Compliance Information: Batch #DS1102PK:
For Further Information contact Rosen Publishing, New York,
New York at 1-800-237-9932

CONTENTS

INTRODUCTION

Welcome to the Monster Fight Club! Watch as people from myth, legend, and history enter the ring to do battle. Have you ever wondered who would win—Vlad the Impaler or Attila the Hun? Find out as you enter the action-packed world of outlaws and villains from history.

How Does It Work?

There are six monster fights in this book. Before each fight, you will see a profile page for each contestant. This page gives you more information about them. Once you have read the profile pages, you might be able to take a better guess at which contestant will win the fight.

WARNING

Blood will be spilled!

The profile pages are crammed with fascinating and bloodcurdling facts about each of the contestants.

The illustrations give background information about the history, life, and times of the contestants.

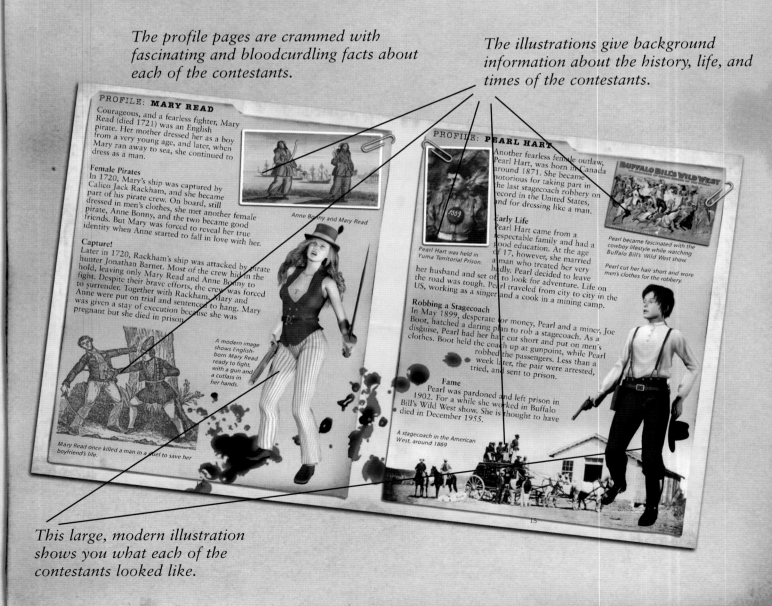

PROFILE: MARY READ

Courageous, and a fearless fighter, Mary Read (died 1721) was an English pirate. Her mother dressed her as a boy from a very young age, and later, when Mary ran away to sea, she continued to dress as a man.

Female Pirates
In 1720, Mary's ship was captured by Calico Jack Rackham, and she became part of his pirate crew. On board, still dressed in men's clothes, she met another female pirate, Anne Bonny, and the two became good friends. But Mary was forced to reveal her true identity when Anne started to fall in love with her.

Capture!
Later in 1720, Rackham's ship was attacked by pirate hunter Jonathan Barnet. Most of the crew hid in the hold, leaving only Mary Read and Anne Bonny to fight. Despite their brave efforts, the crew was forced to surrender. Together with Rackham, Mary and Anne were put on trial and sentenced to hang. Mary was given a stay of execution because she was pregnant but she died in prison.

Anne Bonny and Mary Read

A modern image shows English-born Mary Read ready to fight, with a gun and a cutlass in her hands.

Mary Read once killed a man in a duel to save her boyfriend's life.

PROFILE: PEARL HART

Another fearless female outlaw, Pearl Hart, was born in Canada around 1871. She became notorious for taking part in the last stagecoach robbery on record in the United States, and for dressing like a man.

Early Life
Pearl Hart came from a respectable family and had a good education. At the age of 17, however, she married a man who treated her very badly. Pearl decided to leave her husband and set off to look for adventure. Life on the road was tough. Pearl traveled from city to city in the US, working as a singer and a cook in a mining camp.

Robbing a Stagecoach
In May 1899, desperate for money, Pearl and a miner, Joe Boot, hatched a daring plan to rob a stagecoach. As a disguise, Pearl had her hair cut short and put on men's clothes. Boot held the coach up at gunpoint, while Pearl robbed the passengers. Less than a week later, the pair were arrested, tried, and sent to prison.

Fame
Pearl was pardoned and left prison in 1902. For a while she worked in Buffalo Bill's Wild West show. She is thought to have died in December 1955.

Pearl Hart was held in Yuma Territorial Prison.

Pearl became fascinated with the cowboy lifestyle while watching Buffalo Bill's Wild West show.

Pearl cut her hair short and wore men's clothes for the robbery.

A stagecoach in the American West, around 1869

15

This large, modern illustration shows you what each of the contestants looked like.

In the main text, read a chilling account of how each fight progresses.

Each of the contestants may also fight under a different name, shown here as AKA (Also Known As).

FIGHT 3: MARY READ VS. PEARL HART

Drawn against each other in a duel to the death, the infamous pirate Mary Read and the notorious bandit Pearl Hart face each other under a high noon sun. Both have made names for themselves as brave fighters. Both have honed their skills in a world ruled by men, and have dressed as men since their earliest days. Each recognizes a kindred spirit, but they are also aware of each other's reputations and know that the danger they face is very real.

This is not the first duel that Mary Read has fought and won. And she doesn't suffer fools or cowards lightly. Pearl Hart will have her work cut out for her. Pearl is tough, brave, and armed with a pistol. Trouble is, she has never fired a shot in her life.

Pearl stands facing Mary. To an outsider she appears calm and in control. But Mary is an experienced fighter and recognizes Pearl's fear. She has seen it many times before in her life on the high seas. Taking full advantage of Pearl's slight hesitation, Mary Read unleashes a bone-chilling battle cry and charges straight toward her. Her cutlass is held high in the air in one hand, her blunderbuss in the other.

Faced with such a determined opponent, Pearl lets out a shriek of fear. She is used to robbing stagecoaches, not to fighting a hellcat like Mary. In desperation, she draws her pistol and points it at Mary. Then she pulls the trigger. But the shot only nicks Mary on the arm, sending her into an even greater fury. In turn, she tries to fire her weapon, and Pearl thinks that her time is up. The mechanism on Mary's gun has jammed, and Pearl is unhurt—for now. In the confusion, she has dropped her gun. Before she can reach down and pick it up, Mary has kicked it away. She stands over Pearl, brandishing her cutlass. But Pearl is not quite finished yet. While Mary is distracted by an incoming sandstorm, Pearl turns and runs away. All she can hear as she runs are Mary's shouts of "cowardly cutpurse!" ringing in her ears.

STATS
MARY READ
AKA Mark Read

STRENGTHS: Very fierce and brave fighter. Known to have killed one man in a duel and another when she lost her temper. Can handle pistols, cutlasses, and axes with skill.

WEAKNESSES: Can be outspoken. Heart sometimes rules her head.

STATS
PEARL HART
AKA The Arizona Bandit, Pearl Bywater

STRENGTHS: Carries a .38 revolver with five bullets. Used to being on the run. Toughened by a prison sentence.

WEAKNESSES: Has never fired a shot.

WINNER: MARY READ

At-a-glance STATS boxes give you vital information about each of the contestants, including their main strengths and weaknesses.

The winner's name is given in this black box in the right-hand corner. Of course, you might not agree…

The Monster Fight

After reading the profile pages for each contestant, turn the page to see the fight. Check out the STATS (Statistics) boxes, which give details of the fighters' main strengths and weaknesses. Then read a blow-by-blow account of the battle—if you dare. The winner, if there is one, is shown in a small black box in the bottom right-hand corner.

PROFILE: SPARTACUS

A slave from Thrace (Bulgaria), Spartacus is thought to have lived from about 109–71 BC. Captured by the Romans, he was trained as a gladiator and had many stunning victories in the arena. He later led a rebellion against the Romans.

Gladiators

Gladiators were usually slaves, criminals, or prisoners of war. They were trained in special gladiator schools. A successful gladiator could become a superstar and win his freedom. But most gladiators led short, brutal lives before they were killed in a fight.

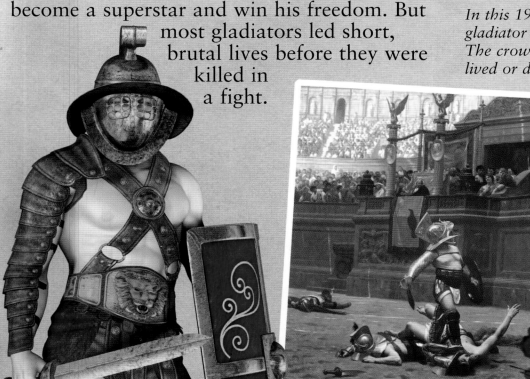

A Roman mosaic showing different types of gladiators. Gladiator fights were held in buildings called amphitheaters. Even though they were gory spectacles, they were hugely popular entertainment in Roman times.

In this 19th-century painting, a defeated gladiator appeals to the crowd for mercy. The crowd had the power to decide if he lived or died.

Spartacus, armed with his gladiator's sword and a shield.

Rebellion

In 73–71 BC, Spartacus led a rebellion against the Romans. It began with a small group of gladiators but grew into an army numbering more than 70,000. When the rebels were finally defeated, some 6,000 were crucified, but Spartacus's body was never found.

PROFILE: **SAIGO TAKAMORI**

One of the greatest Japanese samurai ever, Saigo Takamori was born in 1828. From a humble background, he fought his way to the top, becoming a great leader of the imperial forces. In 1877, Saigo led a rebellion against the central government. He was killed at the Battle of Shiroyama.

Saigo Takamori (1828–1877)

Saigo Takamori (in Western uniform) is shown here surrounded by his officers (wearing traditional samurai armor).

Samurai Warriors

The samurai were traditional Japanese warriors. In battle, they wore spectacular armor and fought with a range of weapons, including bows and arrows, spears, and especially swords.

A samurai warrior was armed with a sword and protected by armor made of lacquered metal plates tied together with leather and silk cords.

Saigo Takamori (upper right) at the Battle of Shiroyama.

Bound by a code of honor, a defeated samurai sometimes chose to commit suicide rather than be captured by the enemy or die a dishonorable death.

Bushido

The samurai led their lives according to a strict code, called Bushido ("Way of the Warrior"). It stressed ways of behaving, such as being loyal to your master, self-discipline, and showing respect.

FIGHT 1: SPARTACUS VS. SAIGO

For today's first fight, two strong opponents step into the arena. The Thracian gladiator, Spartacus, has a grim expression as he snaps his helmet visor shut. A brave and hardened fighter, he has faced this situation many times but he has never been pitted against a contestant like Saigo Takamori before. He will need all his reserves of strength, speed, and courage if he is to overcome the samurai's unshakable sense of honor and superior swordsmanship.

With a roar from the crowd, the contest begins. Both men know that this will be a fight to the death.

STATS
SPARTACUS
AKA Spardacus, Sparadokos

STRENGTHS: Highly trained and successful gladiator. Great leader. Famed for his courage and strength.

WEAKNESSES: Wears only basic armor that cannot withstand blows from the superior samurai sword.

TAKAMORI

STATS
SAIGO TAKAMORI
AKA The Last True Samurai

STRENGTHS: Huge and powerful. Highly skilled swordsman. Bound by Bushido ("Way of the Warrior") code of honor.

WEAKNESSES: Stubborn and rebellious. Never likely to admit defeat.

At first, the two fighters circle each other warily, unwilling to make the first move. The crowd is growing restless. Then, suddenly, Spartacus strikes. Takamori is able to parry a few blows before he is knocked off his feet by Spartacus, who manages to dig his shield under the samurai's chin. The samurai is taken by surprise by Spartacus's aggressive fighting style and is hit with slashing blows that cut through his armor. For a while, it looks as if Spartacus has the upper hand.

But Saigo is not about to give in. A powerful and imposing figure, he is not used to being beaten. With a blood-curdling shriek, he lifts his deadly sword and brings it smashing down on the gladiator, who collapses on the ground. Spartacus raises two fingers to ask for clemency, but the samurai's code of honor does not allow for surrender.

WINNER: SAIGO TAKAMORI

PROFILE: **BLACKBEARD**

Born Edward Teach, in Bristol, England, Blackbeard (c. 1680–1718) was one of the most notorious pirates who ever lived. With his bulging eyes and long, black beard, his fearsome appearance alone was enough to strike terror into his enemies' hearts. Despite his reputation, he commanded his crew well and never harmed his prisoners.

Blackbeard's last fight with the authorities ended with the pirate's death.

Blackbeard's flag showed a skeleton spearing a heart while raising a toast to the Devil.

A modern image of Blackbeard shows him with lighted fuses attached to his beard and hair.

Pirate's Life
In around 1716, Teach captured a ship and renamed it *Queen Anne's Revenge*. For the next two years, he and his crew terrorized ships in the Atlantic Ocean and Caribbean Sea, stealing their cargoes.

The Last Fight
In 1718, Alexander Spotswood, governor of Virginia, decided to end Blackbeard's reign of terror and sent two ships to capture him. After a ferocious last battle, Blackbeard was killed. As a warning, his head was cut off and hung from the bow of one of the ships. The rest of his body was thrown into the sea.

Blackbeard's severed head was hung from the bow of one of the governor's ships.

PROFILE: **ERIK THE RED**

Nicknamed "Erik the Red" because of his flaming red hair, Erik Thorvaldsson (950–c. 1003) had a fiery temper.

A Viking from Norway, legend says that he and his family were involved in some killings at home. To escape punishment, they left Norway and settled in Iceland. Erik was later exiled from Iceland for committing several more murders.

The Vikings were greatly feared warriors as well as skilled seafarers and explorers.

Erik the Red was given his nickname because of his red hair.

The Vikings held meetings, called Things, at which they discussed problems, settled disputes and punished criminals. Erik's punishment was probably decided by a Thing.

Greenland

Erik spent the years of his exile exploring a land to the west of Iceland. He called it Greenland, hoping to encourage other people to go there, and in AD 985, he set off from Iceland with 25 ships filled with settlers and their possessions and livestock. The Vikings established a colony on the southwest coast of Greenland. The climate was warmer than today's, and the colony flourished. Erik, though, died in around 1003 from a disease brought to the island by another group of settlers.

FIGHT 2: BLACKBEARD VS. ERIK THE

Erik the Red stares in amazement and horror at the apparition appearing out of the mist in front of him. As a large figure, with a long, black, smoking beard, advances toward him, Erik is unsure whether it is a man or a devil. Back home, Erik is feared for his temper and has a reputation as a hardened fighter, but he has never come across an opponent like this before. Summoning up his courage, he picks up his ax and charges.

Blackbeard is taken by surprise at the ferocity and speed of Erik's attack. Most of his enemies are not so bold. The pirate's appearance alone is usually enough to strike terror into their hearts and send them fleeing for their lives. But this opponent has shown no fear. As Erik charges, Blackbeard is knocked off balance and drops the pistol he has in his hand. Lightning-fast, Erik smashes his ax down, narrowly missing the rolling Blackbeard. It would seem that the fight is almost over.

STATS
BLACKBEARD
AKA Edward Teach

STRENGTHS: Brave and ruthless fighter. Can take a lot of punishment. Relies on his fearsome appearance to scare enemies. Armed with a cutlass and flintlock pistol.

WEAKNESSES: Burning fuses in his beard can be a hazard. Fond of Madeira wine, which can cloud his sight and judgment.

RED

The smoke coming from the burning fuses in Blackbeard's beard makes it difficult for Erik to see. He finds himself stumbling around, unable to strike the killer blow. Instead, he haphazardly lunges with his ax, giving the pirate time to retrieve his pistol. The tables seem to have turned as Blackbeard picks up his gun and fires at the Viking. But Blackbeard's sight is also blurred by the smoke, and perhaps too much Madeira wine. Unbelievably, he misses.

Erik thinks that the shot is the sound of thunder and believes that the great god Thor is looking out for him. Calling out Thor's name, he launches another vicious attack on Blackbeard. But his newly found confidence is short-lived. Staggering to his feet, Blackbeard steadies himself and gets ready to fire again. This time, he shoots Erik at point-blank range.

STATS
ERIK THE RED
AKA Erik Thorvaldsson

STRENGTHS: Highly skilled fighter. Can take on a number of men single-handed. Trained from childhood to fight with an ax.

WEAKNESSES: Fiery temper. Sometimes acts before he thinks.

WINNER: BLACKBEARD

PROFILE: **MARY READ**

Courageous, and a fearless fighter, Mary Read (died 1721) was an English pirate. Her mother dressed her as a boy from a very young age, and later, when Mary ran away to sea, she continued to dress as a man.

Anne Bonny and Mary Read

Female Pirates

In 1720, Mary's ship was captured by Calico Jack Rackham, and she became part of his pirate crew. On board, still dressed in men's clothes, she met another female pirate, Anne Bonny, and the two became good friends. But Mary was forced to reveal her true identity when Anne started to fall in love with her.

Capture!

Later in 1720, Rackham's ship was attacked by pirate hunter Jonathan Barnet. Most of the crew hid in the hold, leaving only Mary Read and Anne Bonny to fight. Despite their brave efforts, the crew was forced to surrender. Together with Rackham, Mary and Anne were put on trial and sentenced to hang. Mary was given a stay of execution because she was pregnant but she died in prison.

A modern image shows English-born Mary Read ready to fight, with a gun and a cutlass in her hands.

Mary Read once killed a man in a duel to save her boyfriend's life.

PROFILE: **PEARL HART**

Pearl Hart was held in Yuma Territorial Prison.

Another fearless female outlaw, Pearl Hart, was born in Canada around 1871. She became notorious for taking part in the last stagecoach robbery on record in the United States, and for dressing like a man.

Early Life
Pearl Hart came from a respectable family and had a good education. At the age of 17, however, she married a man who treated her very badly. Pearl decided to leave her husband and set off to look for adventure. Life on the road was tough. Pearl traveled from city to city in the US, working as a singer and a cook in a mining camp.

Pearl became fascinated with the cowboy lifestyle while watching Buffalo Bill's Wild West show.

Pearl cut her hair short and wore men's clothes for the robbery.

Robbing a Stagecoach
In May 1899, desperate for money, Pearl and a miner, Joe Boot, hatched a daring plan to rob a stagecoach. As a disguise, Pearl had her hair cut short and put on men's clothes. Boot held the coach up at gunpoint, while Pearl robbed the passengers. Less than a week later, the pair were arrested, tried, and sent to prison.

Fame
Pearl was pardoned and left prison in 1902. For a while she worked in Buffalo Bill's Wild West show. She is thought to have died in December 1955.

A stagecoach in the American West, around 1869

FIGHT 3: MARY READ VS. PEARL HART

Drawn against each other in a duel to the death, the infamous pirate Mary Read and the notorious bandit Pearl Hart face each other under a high noon sun. Both have made names for themselves as brave fighters. Both have honed their skills in a world ruled by men, and have dressed as men since their earliest days. Each recognizes a kindred spirit, but they are also aware of each other's reputations and know that the danger they face is very real.

This is not the first duel that Mary Read has fought and won. And she doesn't suffer fools or cowards lightly. Pearl Hart will have her work cut out for her. Pearl is tough, brave, and armed with a pistol. Trouble is, she has never fired a shot in her life.

STATS

MARY READ
AKA Mark Read

STRENGTHS: Very fierce and brave fighter. Known to have killed one man in a duel and another when she lost her temper. Can handle pistols, cutlasses, and axes with skill.

WEAKNESSES: Can be outspoken. Heart sometimes rules her head.

Pearl stands facing Mary. To an outsider she appears calm and in control. But Mary is an experienced fighter and recognizes Pearl's fear. She has seen it many times before in her life on the high seas. Taking full advantage of Pearl's slight hesitation, Mary Read unleashes a bone-chilling battle cry and charges straight toward her. Her cutlass is held high in the air in one hand, her blunderbuss in the other.

Faced with such a determined opponent, Pearl lets out a shriek of fear. She is used to robbing stagecoaches, not to fighting a hellcat like Mary. In desperation, she draws her pistol and points it at Mary. Then she pulls the trigger. But the shot only nicks Mary on the arm, sending her into an even greater fury. In turn, she tries to fire her weapon, and Pearl thinks that her time is up. The mechanism on Mary's gun has jammed, and Pearl is unhurt—for now. In the confusion, she has dropped her gun. Before she can reach down and pick it up, Mary has kicked it away. She stands over Pearl, brandishing her cutlass. But Pearl is not quite finished yet. While Mary is distracted by an incoming sandstorm, Pearl turns and runs away. All she can hear as she runs are Mary's shouts of "cowardly cutpurse!" ringing in her ears.

WINNER: MARY READ

Vlad the Impaler (1431–1476)

The Prince of Wallachia (Romania), Vlad got his fearsome nickname from his habit of impaling his enemies on stakes. A ruthless ruler, he was said to be a fearless fighter and great leader. He also inspired the legend of the bloodthirsty Count Dracula.

Trained to Rule
Vlad was born in Transylvania in 1431. As a boy, he was sent to the Ottoman (Turkish) court, where he was trained in horseback riding and warfare. In 1448, Vlad became ruler for the first time when his father was killed, but he was soon forced to flee. He returned in 1456 and seized the throne again.

War and Death
During his reign, Vlad fought many bloody battles against the Ottomans, who were trying to claim Wallachia as part of their empire. Legend says that he once had thousands of people impaled on stakes and put on display in order to frighten off the Ottoman army. Vlad was eventually killed on the battlefield in 1476.

A gruesome woodblock showing Vlad eating a meal, surrounded by hundreds of impaled corpses.

Vlad the Impaler in armor, ready to do battle with his archenemy, Mehmet II, ruler of the Ottoman empire.

PROFILE: ATTILA THE HUN

A ruthless fighter and superb horseman, Attila was leader of the mighty Hun empire from 434 until his death in 453. During his rule, he created one of the most formidable armies ever seen and was so feared by his enemies, the Romans, that they called him the Scourge of God. According to a source, Attila was an intelligent man and a great king. But he was also famous for his violent temper and cruelty.

Attila the Hun (c. 410–453)

The Huns

The Huns were nomads from Central Asia who arrived in Europe around 370 BC and built up a huge empire. Under Attila, the Huns reached the height of their power, controlling many of the Roman empire's neighbors. In 442 and 447, he led the Huns against the Roman armies in two massive and savage attacks.

A meeting between Attila and Pope Leo outside Rome

Life and Death

In 452, Attila launched another attack on the Romans, but his army was destroyed by illness and hunger, and he had to make peace. The following year, Attila died. His sons fought over the throne, and this destroyed the Hun empire.

During his rule, Attila was one of the most feared enemies of the Roman empire. A superb warrior, he was skilled at fighting on horseback, especially in close combat with swords.

FIGHT 4: VLAD THE IMPALER VS.

In tonight's fight, two of the true heavyweights of history, Vlad the Impaler and Attila the Hun, come face to face. It is the meeting of two infamous and fearless rulers, both known for their bravery, military power, and their cruelty. The fight will take place on horseback, for both men are superb riders. Both learned to fight for their lives from a very young age, and both excel in close combat. There can only be one winner of this bloody bout, but it is going to be a close call.

The two men circle each other cautiously, sizing up their enemy. Clad in heavy armor, Vlad is slower whereas Attila, whose armor is lighter, is quick and nimble on a smaller horse.

Stats
VLAD THE IMPALER
AKA Vlad III, Prince of Wallachia, Vlad Tepes, Vlad Dracula

STRENGTHS: Fearsome reputation. Showed no mercy to his enemies. Skilled and courageous fighter.

WEAKNESSES: Armor limits movement. Can be jealous and mistrusting.

ATTILA THE HUN

Staying out of reach, Attila, a master archer, fires arrow after arrow at Vlad, but they are no match for Vlad's heavy armor and bounce harmlessly off. Eventually, Attila has no choice. Taking a firm grip on his sword, he closes in for hand-to-hand combat.

STATS
ATTILA THE HUN
AKA Scourge of God

STRENGTHS: Superb archer and javelin thrower. Excellent horseman. Utterly ruthless.

WEAKNESSES: Light, padded armor. Terrible temper.

For a split second, the ferocity of Attila's attack catches Vlad off guard. But he rallies quickly and fights back with some vicious swordwork. Attila tries to use his shield to ward off the blows from Vlad's sword, but the shield is soon smashed to pieces. Realizing that he has met his match, Attila decides to beat a hasty retreat to get reinforcements. Furious, Vlad gives chase but cannot keep up with Attila's speedier horse.

WINNER: VLAD THE IMPALER

PROFILE: **ROBIN HOOD**

A legendary English outlaw, Robin Hood appears in many stories and films as a brilliant archer and gallant hero who robs from the rich to give to the poor. However, no one knows for certain if Robin existed or where he came from.

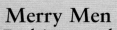

The sheriff of Nottingham (left) was Robin's archenemy.

Merry Men

Robin was leader of a group of fellow outlaws, called the Merry Men. They included Will Scarlet, Friar Tuck, and Little John, Robin's second-in-command and a huge man, despite his nickname. The only woman was Maid Marian, who left her life at the royal court to join Robin.

Robin is said to have met Little John when the two fought a duel.

Sherwood Forest

One legend says that Robin lived in Sherwood Forest near Nottingham, England. He may have been a nobleman who had his lands wrongfully seized by the evil sheriff of Nottingham, who became his archenemy. Some people have suggested that Robin Hood was a general name often used by thieves in those days.

Robin was a skilled swordsman and archer. He used a longbow, made popular in medieval battles (left). Before he died, Robin shot an arrow from his window. Its landing place marked the site of his grave.

PROFILE: **WILLIAM TELL**

Like Robin Hood, William Tell was a rebel who stood up to a local ruler. He was also a superb marksman and an expert shot with a crossbow. A man of the Swiss mountains, William Tell was strong, determined, and brave. He died while trying to save a child from drowning.

In November 1307, William Tell split an apple on his son's head with a bolt from his crossbow.

A Famous Tale

The most famous story about William Tell involves his son and an apple. In 1307, a man named Albrecht Gessler was appointed ruler of the region of Uri, where Tell lived. Gessler put up a pole in the town square and hung his hat from it. The townspeople were told to bow to the hat when they passed. A defiant Tell refused. As punishment, he was ordered to shoot an apple from his son's head, using a crossbow. If he succeeded, he would be set free. If he refused, both he and his son would be killed.

Using his superior archery skills, Tell shot the apple clean in half, without harming his son. But Gessler went back on his word and kept Tell prisoner. Tell managed to escape and later shot Gessler. His actions sparked a rebellion, and he gained a lasting reputation as a heroic freedom fighter.

In 1315, Tell fought against the Austrians at the Battle of Morgarten (below).

A modern image of the folk hero William Tell

This is a crossbow and bolt, which was shorter and heavier than an arrow. Early crossbows were not as effective as longbows, because they took a long time to reload.

FIGHT 5: ROBIN HOOD VS. WILLIAM

The location for tonight's fight is a thickly wooded forest somewhere in Britain. On the run from the authorities, William Tell has taken refuge in the forest, thinking that it will make the perfect hiding place. At first, the forest seems deserted. But as William's eyes slowly grow used to the gloom, he notices a figure standing in the shadows, holding a longbow. William may have escaped his pursuers, but he has stumbled across a far greater foe. The shadowy figure is none other than Robin Hood, fearless outlaw and, like William himself, expert marksman. The stage is set for a stunning showdown.

They begin their fight at a distance. Robin's longbow is quick to reload, but it is difficult to hit a fast-moving target among the trees. William's crossbow is more accurate but takes much longer to reload, allowing Robin to move in closer. More arrows fly, but the fight soon reaches a stalemate. The two opponents are perfectly matched. Both are brave fighters. Both have spent much of their lives in hiding and are used to biding their time. Eventually, growing frustrated, William resorts to tricks. He tries to lure Robin out by pretending that he has Maid Marian captive, but his ploy fails.

Finally, Robin has fired his last arrow and is caught in the open. William takes aim and is about to shoot when an apple falls from a tree. Out of habit, he takes aim and fires. Realizing that he has shot his last bolt and is at a disadvantage since Robin has a sword, William turns and runs away.

STATS
ROBIN HOOD
AKA Earl of Huntingdon

STRENGTHS: Highly skilled swordsman; expert at hand-to-hand fighting. Excellent shot with a longbow. Gallant and brave.

WEAKNESSES: Always on the run from the law for robbery and other crimes. Has the sheriff of Nottingham as his archenemy.

STATS
WILLIAM TELL
AKA Wilhelm Tell

STRENGTHS: Expert marksman with a crossbow. Strong and determined.

WEAKNESSES: Crossbow has slow reload time. Sometimes reacts to events without thinking first.

WINNER: ROBIN HOOD

PROFILE: NED KELLY

Born around 1855, Ned Kelly had a tough childhood and was regularly in trouble with the police. Daring and brave, he went on to become Australia's most infamous outlaw.

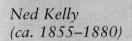

*Ned Kelly
(ca. 1855–1880)*

The gang's armor was made of metal and still survives.

Outlaw

In April 1878 a policeman claimed that he had been shot in the hand by Ned and his gang. Although the man's story was most likely untrue, Ned and his brother went on the run. The police sent a search party to hunt them down, and three policemen were killed in a skirmish. Ned was declared an outlaw, meaning that anyone could shoot him.

Final Shoot-Out

Two years later, Ned fought his final battle. Wearing homemade metal armor, the Kelly Gang faced police in a shoot-out at Glenrowan. Ned was captured and sent to prison. He was hanged for murder in November 1880.

Life on the run in the Australian outback was very tough.

Ned Kelly wearing his homemade armor as he might have appeared before the Glenrowan shoot-out

PROFILE: **BILLY THE KID**

Henry McCarty, aka Billy the Kid, was born in New York City on September 17, 1859. He and his gang became notorious outlaws of the American Old West, though legend may have exaggerated his feats. During his lifetime, he was said to have killed more than 20 men, though the true number may be closer to 9.

Outlaw and Killer

As a teenager, Billy stole horses and killed a man. He was arrested but escaped. He found work with a man named John Tunstall, who was later murdered. Billy vowed to take revenge for the murder and he and his gang set off on a killing spree. Again, Billy managed to escape from the police and returned to stealing.

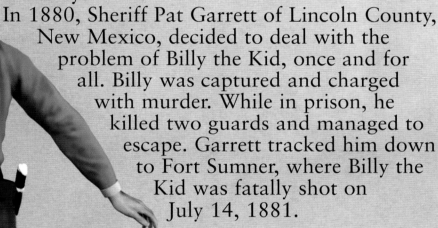

A modern image of Billy the Kid

Final Days

In 1880, Sheriff Pat Garrett of Lincoln County, New Mexico, decided to deal with the problem of Billy the Kid, once and for all. Billy was captured and charged with murder. While in prison, he killed two guards and managed to escape. Garrett tracked him down to Fort Sumner, where Billy the Kid was fatally shot on July 14, 1881.

These photographs show Billy the Kid (above) and Sheriff Pat Garrett, who shot him down (below).

Revolvers like this were popular in the 1800s.

A cowboy in the Old West in the 1880s

FIGHT 6: NED KELLY VS. BILLY

The final fight of the day takes place on a bleak and windswept plain, where a strange quirk of fate has brought together two of history's most infamous outlaws. In the far corner is the battle-hardened figure of Australian outlaw Ned Kelly, dressed in homemade armor worn under a long coat. Facing him, in the near corner, stands Henry McCarty, better known as Billy the Kid.

On the run after killing a policeman, Kelly is a desperate man, and he is in a hurry. He is certainly in no mood to be crossed or delayed. He looks at the boyish figure in front of him and shakes his head. He doesn't think much of his opponent and will soon have him beaten, or so he supposes. He picks up his rifle, takes aim, and just then, he feels a searing pain shooting down his arm and yells out with surprise. The Kid has fired a shot that has hit Kelly on the hand.

STATS
NED KELLY
AKA Edward Kelly

STRENGTHS: Daring and used to a hard life. Homemade armor is bulletproof.

WEAKNESSES: Can be a cold-blooded killer. Slit in helmet makes it difficult to see.

THE KID

Kelly holds his rifle in his uninjured hand and lurches toward the Kid, ready to fire. Realizing his disadvantage, the Kid uses some nimble footwork to dodge around the lumbering Kelly. He also tries to keep a safe distance away. Now that Kelly has only one good hand, his aim is wild. Ned's armor is also making it difficult for Billy. Although he's a great shot, he can't hit his target—the slit in Ned's metal helmet.

Finally, Billy realizes that Ned's armor doesn't cover his legs. With his last bullet, he disables Ned by shooting him in the leg. Ned falls to the ground, faint from the loss of blood, and victory goes to the Kid.

STATS
BILLY THE KID
AKA Henry McCarty, Henry Antrim, William H. Bonney

STRENGTHS: Excellent with revolver. Very light on his feet. Cunning and charismatic.

WEAKNESSES: Small and slight, so no good in a brawl.

WINNER: BILLY THE KID

29

CREATE YOUR OWN FIGHT

You might not agree with some of the fight results in this book. If that's the case, why not write up your own fight report based on the facts supplied on the prefight profile pages? Better still, choose your own outlaws or villains and create your own monster fight.

Monster Research
Once you have chosen your two outlaws or villains, do some research about them using books and the Internet. You can make them fairly similar, like Robin Hood and William Tell, or quite different, like Spartacus and Saigo Takamori.

Stats Boxes
Think about stats for each contestant. Find out about any other names for the AKA section. Make a list of strengths, such as whether they wear armor, what type of weapons they use, and any specialties, like being a great shot. Then write a list of their weaknesses.

In the Ring
Pick a setting where your contestants are likely to meet, and write a blow-by-blow account of how you imagine the fight might happen. Try to include as many of their strengths and weaknesses as you can. Remember, the loser doesn't have to die!

Outlaws and Villains from History
This list includes some other outlaws and villains that might become members in the Monster Fight Club.

Anne Bonny
Butch Cassidy
Calico Jack Rackham
Captain Kidd
Dick Turpin
Elizabeth Bathory
Genghis Khan
Henry Morgan
Ivan the Terrible
Jesse James
Lucrezia Borgia
Matthew Hopkins
Pancho Villa
The Sundance Kid

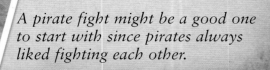

A pirate fight might be a good one to start with since pirates always liked fighting each other.

GLOSSARY

amphitheaters (AMP-fuh-thee-eh-terz)
Circular or oval buildings with an open, central arena in which the Romans staged gladiator fights.

aristocrat (uh-RIS-tuh-krat)
A noble or person from a privileged background.

bow (BOW)
The forward end or part of a ship.

Bushido (BUH-shih-doh)
Bushido was a strict code of behavior, which samurai warriors followed in their lives. It means "way of the warrior."

crucified (KROO-suh-fyd)
When someone was put to death by being nailed or tied to a cross by their hands and feet.

cutlass (KUT-lus)
A curved, one-edged sword once used by pirates.

duel (DOO-el)
A fight between two contestants, armed with deadly weapons, usually to settle a quarrel.

famine (FA-men)
A very serious shortage of food because crops fail or there are too many people to feed.

fuses (FYOOZ-ez)
Twists of gunpowder or explosives which the pirate Blackbeard put in his beard.

imperial (im-PEER-ee-ul)
To do with an empire or an emperor.

lacquered (LA-kerd)
Decorated with a hard, glossy coating.

mosaic (moh-ZAY-ik)
A picture made up of tiny pieces of colored glass or stone. The Romans were famous for their mosaics.

nomads (NOH-madz)
People who move from place to place, looking for food, water, and grazing for their animals.

outlaw (OWT-law)
A person who has committed a crime and is on the run from the law.

samurai (SA-muh-ry)
A traditional Japanese warrior, famous for his armor, bravery, and code of honor.

scourge (SKURJ)
A person who causes great destruction.

stagecoach (STAYJ-kohch)
A large, four-wheeled horsedrawn vehicle, used to carry passengers and mail on a regular route.

stay of execution (STAY UV ek-suh-KYOO-shun)
When a criminal's execution is delayed or put on hold for some reason.

INDEX

Web Sites

Due to the changing nature of Internet links, PowerKids Press has developed an online list of Web sites related to the subject of this book. This site is updated regularly. Please use this link to access the list:
www.powerkidslinks.com/mfc/outlaws/